A Random House TELL ME ABOUT Book

THE HUMAN BODY
& HOW IT WORKS

By Angela Royston
Illustrated by Rob Shone
& Chris Forsey

D1397122

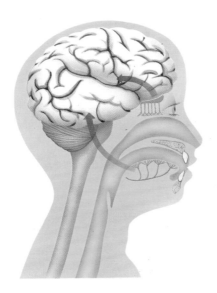

Random House 🏠 New York

First American edition, 1991

Library of Congress Cataloging-in-Publication Data
Royston, Angela.
    The human body & how it works / by Angela
Royston; illustrated by Rob Shone & Chris
Forsey.
        p.   cm.—(Tell me about)
    Includes index.
    Summary: Questions and answers introduce
the human body and how it works.
    ISBN 0-679-80860-4
    1. Human physiology—Juvenile literature.
2. Human anatomy—Juvenile literature.
3. Body, Human—Juvenile literature. [1. Human
anatomy—Miscellanea. 2. Body, Human—
Miscellanea 3. Questions and answers.] I. Shone,
Rob, ill. II. Forsey, Christopher, ill. III. Title.
IV. Title: Human body and how it works.
V. Series.
QP37.R78 1991
612—dc20   90-42978
                                          CIP
                                           AC
Manufactured in Spain   1 2 3 4 5 6 7 8 9 10

Contents

What are our bodies made of?

Our bodies are made of millions of tiny living units called cells, most of them too small to be seen without a microscope. These cells are the building blocks from which everything else is made – bones, blood, muscles, skin, and all the other parts of the body. There are many different kinds of cells, and each type has its own special job to do.

BODY FACTS

● Your body is mainly made of water – water accounts for 70% of your weight, in fact.

● Your heart is a muscle which pumps blood around your body. An adult's heart beats over 100,000 times each day.

● Cells come in all shapes and sizes – some are round, some are flat, some are square. Most cells have a control center called a nucleus, which keeps the cell alive and doing its own special job. New cells are made when one cell divides.

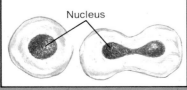

Nucleus

? DO YOU KNOW

The average human body has enough iron in it to make a nail nearly 1 inch long, and enough phosphorus to make over 2,000 match heads. It also contains the same amount of carbon as 28 pounds of the fuel coke, and more than 2 pounds of calcium (also found in chalk).

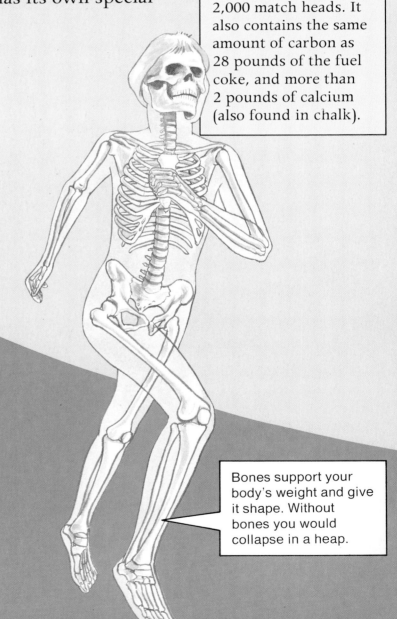

Bones support your body's weight and give it shape. Without bones you would collapse in a heap.

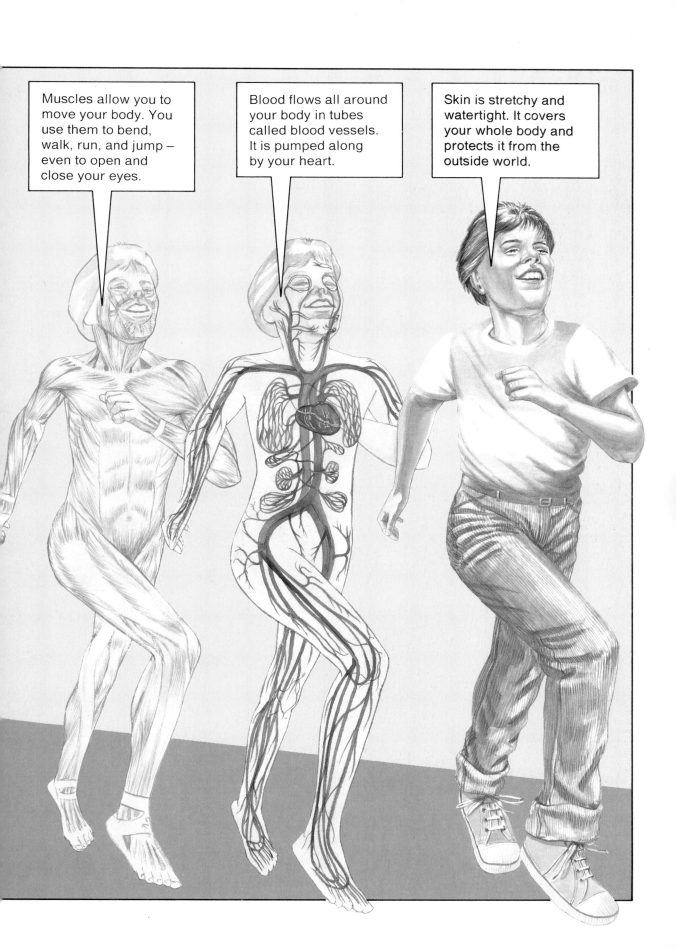

How many bones do we have?

By the time we are fully grown we have about 206 different bones, but when we were born we had around 350. This is because many smaller bones join together as we grow.

Bones make a framework called the skeleton, which supports the body and carries its weight. Some bones also protect important parts of the body from being injured – the skull protects the brain, for example.

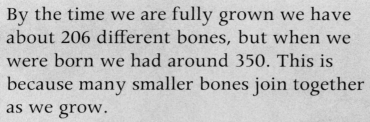

There are 26 bones in each foot. They are put together like the hand bones, but toes can't move as freely as fingers can.

Kneecap (patella)

Thighbone (femur)

Shinbone (tibia)

Fibula

Each leg has three long leg bones – one above the kneecap bone and two below it. They carry the whole weight of the body.

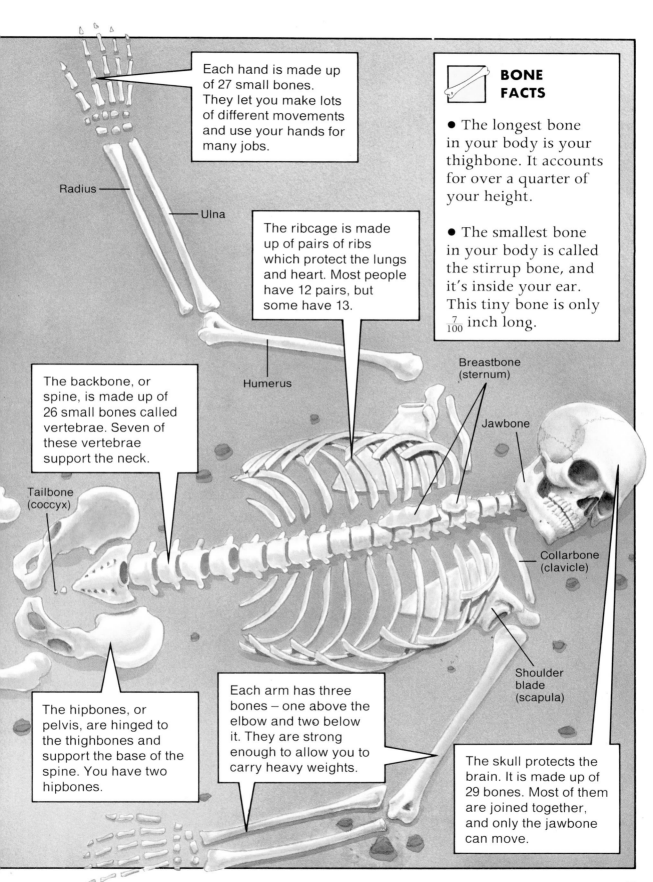

Each hand is made up of 27 small bones. They let you make lots of different movements and use your hands for many jobs.

Radius

Ulna

The ribcage is made up of pairs of ribs which protect the lungs and heart. Most people have 12 pairs, but some have 13.

Humerus

The backbone, or spine, is made up of 26 small bones called vertebrae. Seven of these vertebrae support the neck.

Breastbone (sternum)

Jawbone

Tailbone (coccyx)

Collarbone (clavicle)

The hipbones, or pelvis, are hinged to the thighbones and support the base of the spine. You have two hipbones.

Each arm has three bones – one above the elbow and two below it. They are strong enough to allow you to carry heavy weights.

Shoulder blade (scapula)

The skull protects the brain. It is made up of 29 bones. Most of them are joined together, and only the jawbone can move.

What are bones like inside?

Our bones are hard and strong because they are partly made of a stony material. Unlike stones, though, bones are neither solid nor dead. They are more like strong tubes which carry blood and other living material inside them. Bones are made by living cells, and they can grow and repair themselves if they get cracked or broken.

DO YOU KNOW

Newborn babies' bones are softer than ours. This is because bones start off as soft bendy stuff called cartilage. As we grow, most of it turns into hard bone, but our noses and ears still have cartilage in them.

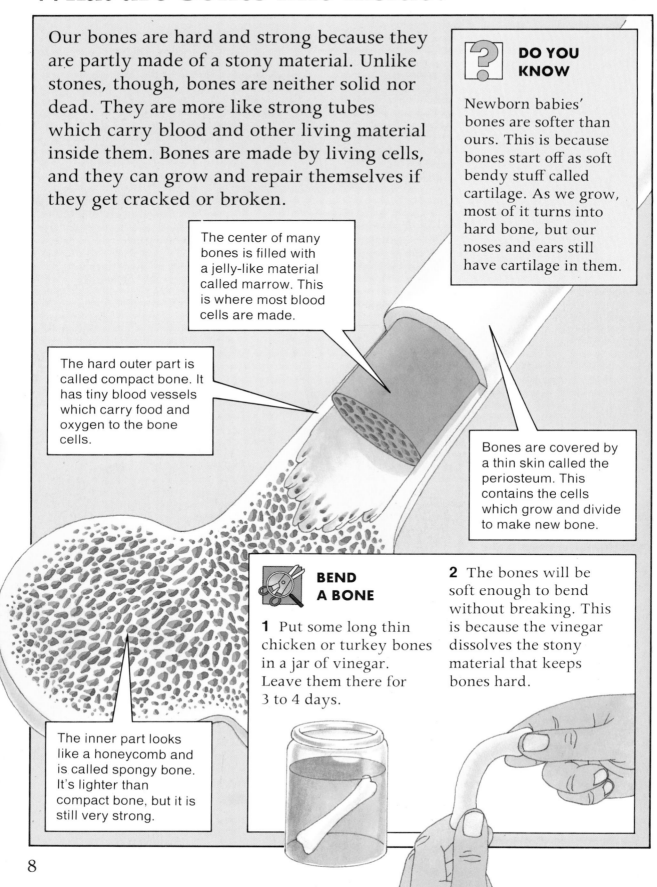

The center of many bones is filled with a jelly-like material called marrow. This is where most blood cells are made.

The hard outer part is called compact bone. It has tiny blood vessels which carry food and oxygen to the bone cells.

Bones are covered by a thin skin called the periosteum. This contains the cells which grow and divide to make new bone.

The inner part looks like a honeycomb and is called spongy bone. It's lighter than compact bone, but it is still very strong.

BEND A BONE

1 Put some long thin chicken or turkey bones in a jar of vinegar. Leave them there for 3 to 4 days.

2 The bones will be soft enough to bend without breaking. This is because the vinegar dissolves the stony material that keeps bones hard.

How do joints work?

The place where two bones meet is called a joint. Some bones are fixed firmly together – the ones in the skull, for example – but our bodies also have several kinds of movable joints. These joints allow us to bend, twist, and turn various parts of our bodies. Two of the main kinds of movable joints are illustrated below.

 DO YOU KNOW

Many joints are "oiled" with a liquid called synovial fluid to help them move. The bone heads are cushioned with cartilage and held in place by elastic straps called ligaments.

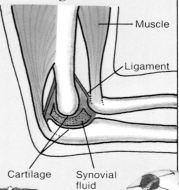

Muscle
Ligament
Cartilage
Synovial fluid

Did you know that you are about $\frac{1}{2}$ inch shorter in the evening than when you wake in the morning? Each of the 26 bones in your spine is separated by a disk, or pad, of cartilage. As you walk around during the day, the weight of your upper body squashes the disks – this is what makes you a little shorter by the time evening comes.

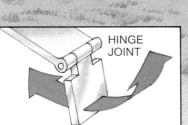

HINGE JOINT

Your elbows and knees have hinge joints. Joints like these bend and straighten just like a door swinging on its hinges.

BALL-AND-SOCKET JOINT

In a ball-and-socket joint, the round end of one bone fits into a hollow in another bone. Shoulders and hips have ball-and-socket joints.

What jobs do muscles do?

All the movements our bodies make depend on muscles – even when we are standing still, we are using muscles in our backs, necks, arms, and legs to stay upright. Many of our muscles work without our thinking about them, like the ones we use in breathing and in digesting our food.

Most things we do take many muscles working together. This is because muscles can't push, they can only pull. You can see how muscles work together in the diagram opposite.

MUSCLE FACTS

● Your body has more than 650 muscles.

● You use 200 muscles every time you take a step.

● There are more than 30 muscles in your face. It takes 15 muscles to smile.

The weight lifter bends his knees and positions his feet apart, so that he can use his leg and back muscles as well as his arms to help lift and carry the weight of the dumbbell.

Weight lifters need very powerful muscles. Exercise makes muscles bigger and stronger.

Because muscles can only pull, not push, they often work in pairs. One muscle shortens to pull a bone one way, then another muscle pulls the bone back again.

Biceps muscle

Radius bone

1

Muscles are attached to bones by tendons.

1 To bend the arm, the biceps shortens and pulls up the radius bone.

2 To straighten the arm, the biceps relaxes and the triceps shortens.

2

Biceps muscle

Triceps muscle

Doctors use Latin names to identify different muscles.

Deltoid (shoulder)

Latissimus dorsi (rib)

Sternomastoid (neck)

Pectoralis major (breast)

Rectus abdominis (stomach)

Rectus femoris (thigh)

Gastrocnemius (calf)

Sartorius (inner thigh)

Peroneus brevis (ankle)

DO YOU KNOW

We all have muscles for wiggling our ears! There is one behind each ear, but most of us never learn to use it. We can't wiggle our ears because muscles that don't get exercised become weak and can't be used.

11

How fast can people run?

The fastest race is the 100-meter dash, and the best male runners can finish it in less than 10 seconds – that's 22 miles per hour (mph). The fastest women runners take just over half a second longer.

RUNNING FACTS

● In l954, Roger Bannister of Great Britain became the first person to run a mile in less than 4 minutes. Bannister's actual time was 3 minutes 59.4 seconds.

● The longest race is the marathon, with a distance of 26.2 miles. The fastest marathon runners average nearly 12.5 mph.

How high can people jump?

The best high jumpers can jump more than their own height – well over 7 feet. They use the Fosbury flop, the technique shown below, which was invented by Dick Fosbury in 1968. Using a pole helps the best pole-vaulters to clear about 19 feet.

To cushion their fall, high jumpers land on deep padded mats or air-filled mattresses.

For the Fosbury flop, the high jumper turns his back to the bar. He arches his back over the bar as he jumps, and kicks his legs out to clear it. He lands on the mat on his shoulders and his back.

How far can people jump?

In l968, Bob Beamon jumped 29 feet during the Olympic Games in Mexico City. This record has stood for more than 20 years. The women's long jump record is 24 feet $8\frac{1}{4}$ inches.

Long jumpers run up to a takeoff board and jump into a pit filled with sand. The faster the run-up, the better the jump.

GAMES FACTS

- The modern Olympic Games began in l896. They are now held every four years.

- There are 31 sports – 23 in the Summer Games and 8 in the Winter Games.

- In 1972, US swimmer Mark Spitz became the first competitor to win 7 gold medals in one Olympics.

How fast can people swim?

The fastest male swimmers can cover 164 feet in a swimming pool in under 23 seconds – that's 4.8 mph. The fastest women swimmers take about 3 seconds longer. To go this fast, swimmers use a stroke called freestyle.

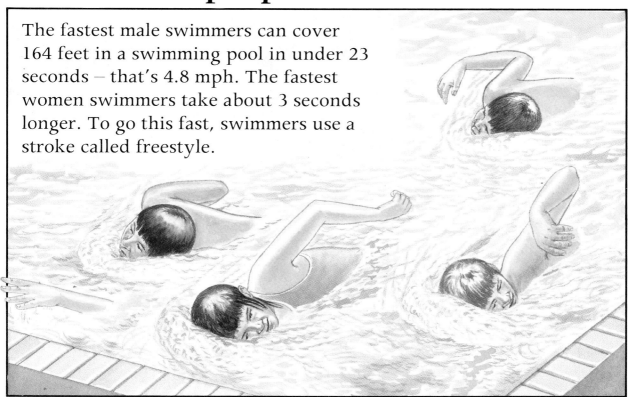

Why do we breathe?

When we breathe air into our lungs, our bodies take a gas called oxygen from it. The oxygen passes from the lungs into the blood and is then carried around the body. Body cells need oxygen to make energy – if cells are starved of oxygen, they run out of energy and die. We all need the oxygen in air to stay alive.

BREATHING FACTS

● We take in 23,000 breaths every day.

● An adult's lungs hold 5 quarts of air.

1 When you breathe in, air is drawn through your nose or mouth and down your windpipe. The air is warmed on the way.

2 Your windpipe branches into two bronchial tubes – one for each lung. Inside the lungs, the tubes divide again and again, becoming smaller and smaller.

You have two lungs, one in each side of your chest. You can feel them fill with air as you breathe in.

Lungs

3 The tiniest tubes in your lungs end in bunches of air sacs called alveoli. Each air sac is surrounded by tiny blood vessels. The air sacs and blood vessels have such thin walls that oxygen can pass through them into the blood.

Alveoli

Blood vessels

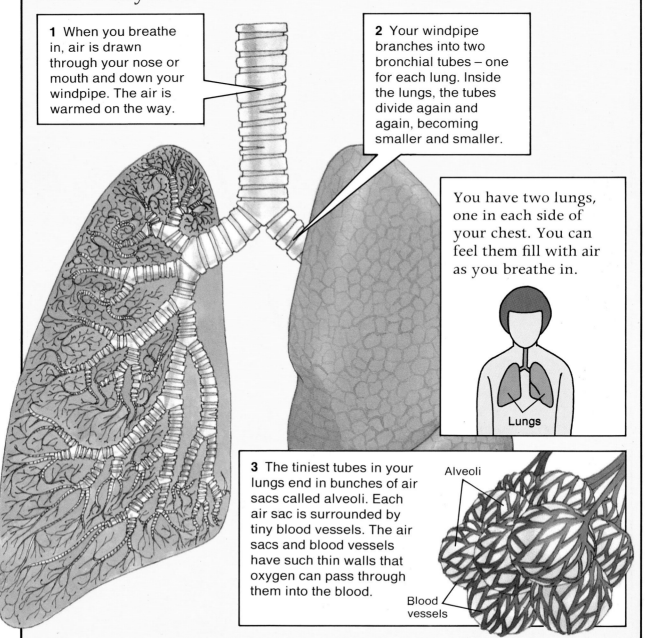

What are hiccups?

Hiccups are short, sharp, and very sudden breaths of air. They happen when our breathing muscle jerks, making us gasp. Our lungs have no muscles of their own. Instead, they have a big muscle called the diaphragm below them. When the diaphragm pulls down, air is sucked into the lungs. When it relaxes, it pushes air out.

DO YOU KNOW

When you sneeze, air rushes down your nose at over 100 mph. You can't sneeze with your eyes open!

MEASURE YOUR BREATH

1 Ask an adult to help you fill an empty 2-quart bottle with water, 3 ounces at a time. Mark each level on the side of the bottle.

2 Cover the top of the bottle and turn it upside down in a bowl which is half-full of water.

3 Put one end of a length of plastic tube into the neck of the bottle. Take a deep breath, then blow into the tube. How much water can your breath push out of the bottle?

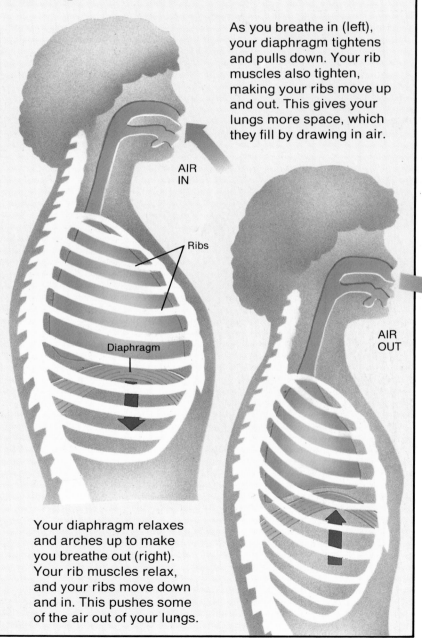

AIR IN

Ribs

Diaphragm

AIR OUT

As you breathe in (left), your diaphragm tightens and pulls down. Your rib muscles also tighten, making your ribs move up and out. This gives your lungs more space, which they fill by drawing in air.

Your diaphragm relaxes and arches up to make you breathe out (right). Your rib muscles relax, and your ribs move down and in. This pushes some of the air out of your lungs.

Why is blood red?

Although blood looks red, it is largely made up of a yellowish liquid called plasma. Different sorts of blood cells float in the plasma – red cells, white cells, and tiny bits of cell called platelets. The red blood cells contain a substance called hemoglobin, which is the body's oxygen carrier. It is hemoglobin which gives red cells their color and makes blood look red.

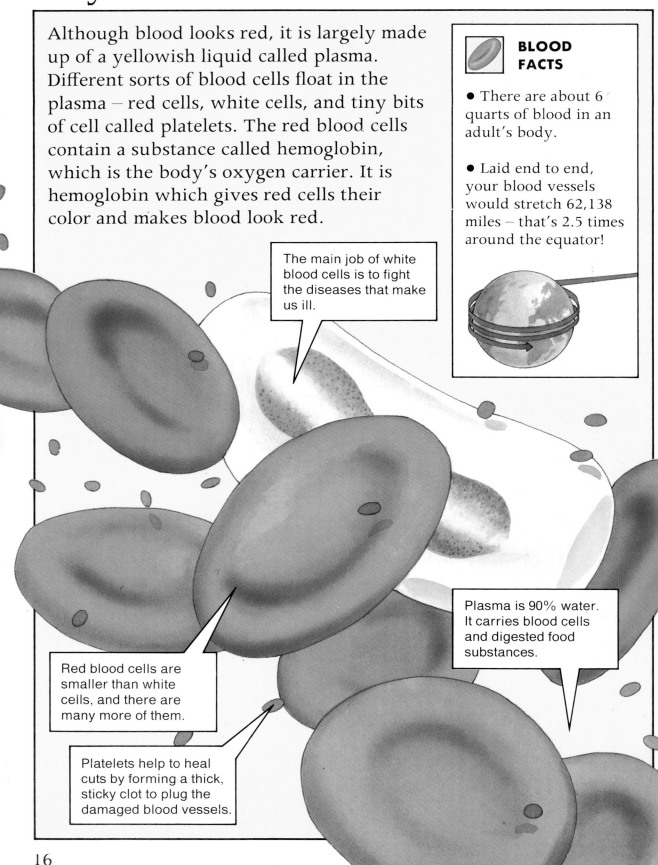

BLOOD FACTS

● There are about 6 quarts of blood in an adult's body.

● Laid end to end, your blood vessels would stretch 62,138 miles – that's 2.5 times around the equator!

The main job of white blood cells is to fight the diseases that make us ill.

Plasma is 90% water. It carries blood cells and digested food substances.

Red blood cells are smaller than white cells, and there are many more of them.

Platelets help to heal cuts by forming a thick, sticky clot to plug the damaged blood vessels.

How do cuts heal?

As soon as your skin is cut or grazed, your body starts to repair it. The platelets in your blood rush to block breaks in the blood vessels just below the surface of the skin. They thicken and clot the blood, making it lumpy and plugging the breaks. The bleeding stops and the blood hardens into a scab. New skin cells then grow through the wound, and after a while the scab falls off.

DO YOU KNOW

Bruises form when blood vessels break and bleed under the skin – if you bump yourself, for example, but your skin isn't cut. As the blood clears away, the bruise turns from black to purple to yellow.

1 When you bleed, the blood helps to clean the wound. The bleeding will stop as platelets make the blood clot.

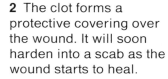

2 The clot forms a protective covering over the wound. It will soon harden into a scab as the wound starts to heal.

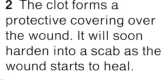

3 New skin cells will grow under the scab. The new skin will look pink at first – you'll see it when the scab falls off.

DO YOU KNOW

People have different types of blood. There are four groups in all – A, B, AB, and O. Blood groups are important when patients are given blood transfusions. People are usually given blood that matches their own blood type.

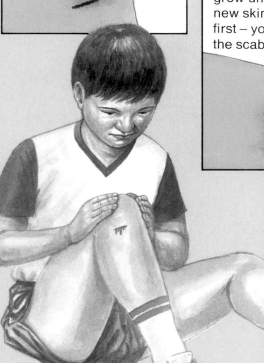

What does the heart do?

Your heart is a powerful muscle which pumps blood around your body, so that each cell gets the food and oxygen it needs. The left-hand side of the heart draws in oxygen-filled blood from the lungs and pushes it out again, around the body. The right-hand side takes in "used" blood and sends it to the lungs to pick up a fresh supply of oxygen. Blood enters the heart in vessels called veins, and leaves it in arteries.

 DO YOU KNOW

An adult human's heart usually beats about 70 times a minute. A mouse's heart beats about 500 times a minute, but an elephant's heart beats only about 25 times a minute!

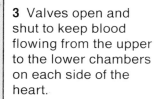

 LISTEN TO HEARTBEATS

1 Ask an adult to help you take the spout off an empty detergent bottle and cut off the top of the bottle.

2 Push the end of a piece of plastic tubing over the neck of the bottle top.

3 Put the bottle top over a friend's heart, and hold the other end of the tube close to your ear. Can you hear a lub-dub lub-dub sound? It's made by the heart valves opening and shutting.

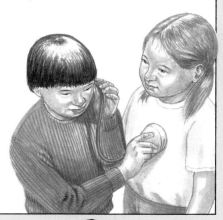

2 The blood flows from the vena cava into the upper right-hand chamber of the heart. This part is called the right atrium.

3 Valves open and shut to keep blood flowing from the upper to the lower chambers on each side of the heart.

 DO YOU KNOW

Your heart is about the same size as your clenched fist. It's protected by your ribs and breastbone.

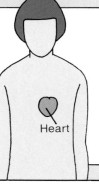

Heart

4 The lower right-hand chamber of the heart is called the right ventricle. From here, the "used" blood is pumped to the lungs.

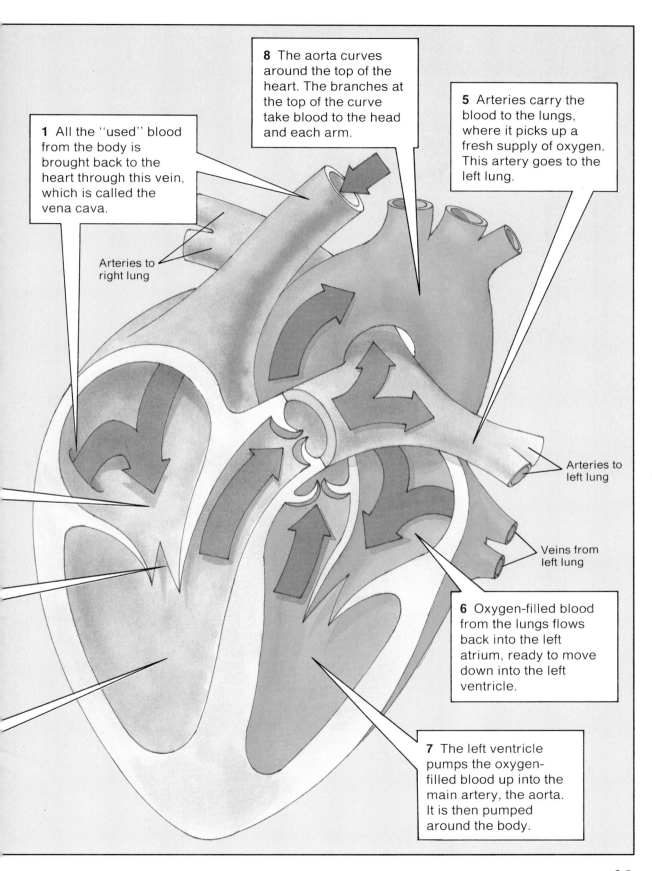

8 The aorta curves around the top of the heart. The branches at the top of the curve take blood to the head and each arm.

5 Arteries carry the blood to the lungs, where it picks up a fresh supply of oxygen. This artery goes to the left lung.

1 All the "used" blood from the body is brought back to the heart through this vein, which is called the vena cava.

Arteries to right lung

Arteries to left lung

Veins from left lung

6 Oxygen-filled blood from the lungs flows back into the left atrium, ready to move down into the left ventricle.

7 The left ventricle pumps the oxygen-filled blood up into the main artery, the aorta. It is then pumped around the body.

19

What do kidneys do?

Kidneys clean the blood by filtering out waste matter and straining off any water your body doesn't need. This liquid waste is called urine. It leaves your body when you go to the bathroom.

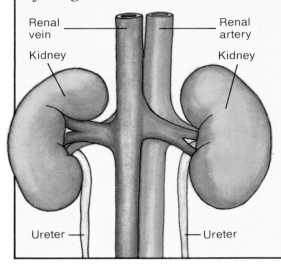

Renal vein

Renal artery

Kidney

Kidney

Ureter

Ureter

1 Blood from the heart is pumped through the renal artery to each kidney to be cleaned.

2 Filtered blood flows through the renal vein back to the heart.

3 Urine slowly drips through tubes called ureters to the bladder, where it is stored until you go to the bathroom.

You have two kidneys, one on either side of your backbone at about waist level. They look like large reddish brown beans. Each one is roughly the size of your clenched fist.

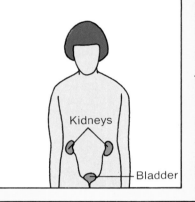

Kidneys

Bladder

Why do we chew food?

We chew food to make it easier to swallow and to help our stomachs to digest it. We use our front teeth to bite into food. As our back teeth grind up the food, it mixes with saliva and becomes soft and mushy.

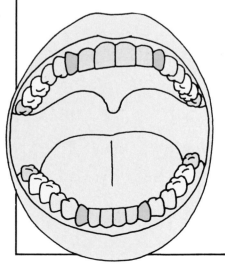

Different teeth do different jobs. The ones at the front of the mouth are sharp and shaped like knives, for cutting. The back ones are wide and bumpy, for grinding.

Incisors – for cutting and grinding

Canines – for cutting and tearing

Premolars ⎤ for crunching
Molars ⎦ and grinding

Wisdom teeth

 ACID ATTACK

Sugar left in your mouth after eating turns to acid, which then attacks your teeth. Eggshells are made of similar stuff to teeth. Drop a shell in vinegar (an acid) and leave it for a few days. What happens?

What happens to the food we eat?

After you swallow it, food travels through the part of your body called the digestive system. This includes your stomach and your intestines. Substances in the digestive system break the food down into simple chemicals, which are small enough to pass into your blood to feed your body cells.

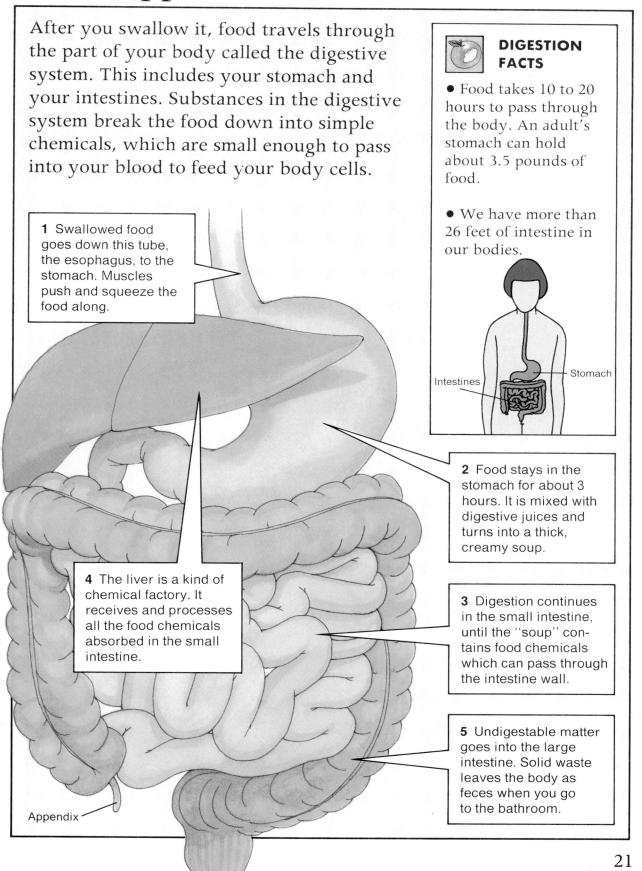

DIGESTION FACTS

● Food takes 10 to 20 hours to pass through the body. An adult's stomach can hold about 3.5 pounds of food.

● We have more than 26 feet of intestine in our bodies.

Intestines — Stomach

1 Swallowed food goes down this tube, the esophagus, to the stomach. Muscles push and squeeze the food along.

4 The liver is a kind of chemical factory. It receives and processes all the food chemicals absorbed in the small intestine.

Appendix

2 Food stays in the stomach for about 3 hours. It is mixed with digestive juices and turns into a thick, creamy soup.

3 Digestion continues in the small intestine, until the "soup" contains food chemicals which can pass through the intestine wall.

5 Undigestable matter goes into the large intestine. Solid waste leaves the body as feces when you go to the bathroom.

What does the brain do?

The brain is the body's control center. It keeps the different parts of the body working smoothly, and it is responsible for thoughts, feelings, and memory.

The brain is linked to the rest of the body by nerves. These work like telephone wires, sending information to the brain in the form of tiny electrical currents. The brain sifts the information and acts on some of it by sending instructions back along the nerves.

 DO YOU KNOW

A large bundle of nerve cells runs from the brain down the back inside the backbone. It's called the spinal cord. Smaller nerves run from the spinal cord to the rest of the body.

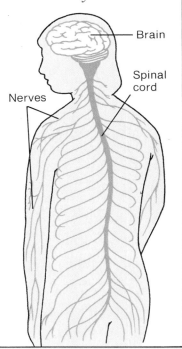

Brain

Spinal cord

Nerves

 KNEE JERKER

We do some things without thinking about them – if we touch something very hot, for example, our hands jerk away. This kind of response is called a reflex action. It's when the body reacts without waiting for a message from the brain. Here's a way of comparing reflex actions with ordinary responses.

1 Sit with your legs crossed and ask a friend to tap gently just below your kneecap. When your friend taps the right spot, your foot will jerk up. This is a reflex action.

2 Now have your friend just *ask* you to jerk your foot. The jerk will take longer because the message has to travel farther – from your ears via your brain to your muscles.

 BRAIN FACTS

● An adult's brain weighs about 3 pounds and has 14 billion nerve cells in it.

● The fastest messages pass along the nerves at speeds of 250 mph.

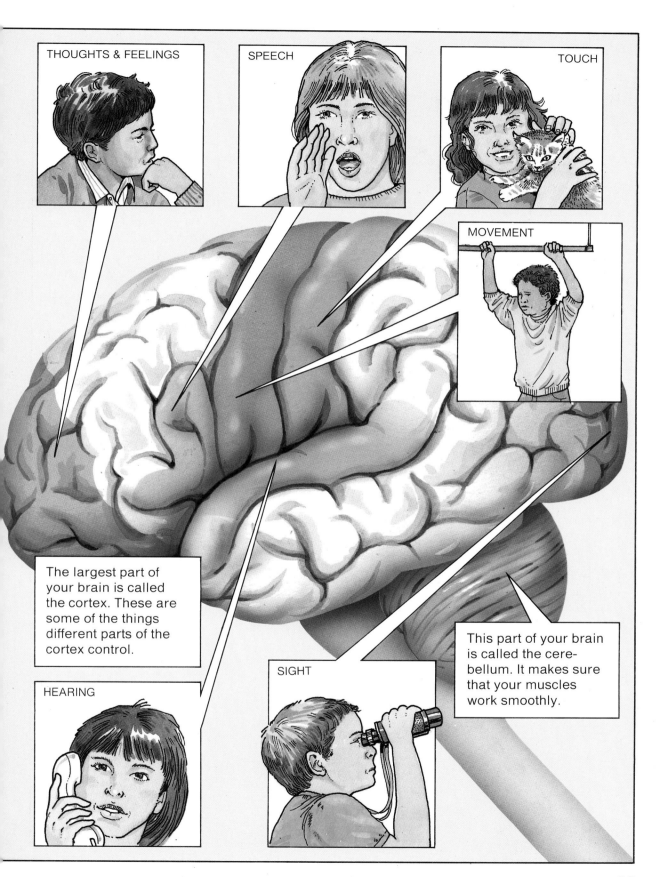

THOUGHTS & FEELINGS

SPEECH

TOUCH

MOVEMENT

The largest part of your brain is called the cortex. These are some of the things different parts of the cortex control.

This part of your brain is called the cerebellum. It makes sure that your muscles work smoothly.

HEARING

SIGHT

How do eyes work?

Eyes work like cameras do, only much faster. Both need light, and both have lenses to make images as clear and sharp as possible. Instead of the film in a camera, however, the back of each eye has a special lining called the retina. The retina contains cells which are sensitive to light. Messages from these cells travel along nerves to your brain, which then makes a picture in your mind.

 EYE FACTS

● An adult's eyeball is about as big as a Ping-Pong ball. A jelly-like material inside the eyeball keeps its shape, like the air in a balloon.

● There are about 132 million light-sensitive cells in the retina of each eye.

The retina lines the back of the eyeball. Light-sensitive cells in the retina send messages along the optic nerve to the brain.

There aren't any light-sensitive cells at the point where the optic nerve enters the eye. This point is called the blind spot.

The black centers of your eyes are holes which let in light. They're called pupils. The colored ring around the pupil is called the iris.

The lens focuses, or sharpens, the image you are looking at, so that a clear picture forms on the retina.

Optic nerve to brain

 FIND YOUR BLIND SPOT

1 Cover your left eye and look at the hat.

2 Move the book toward you – the rabbit will disappear!

What happens when we cry?

Did you know that your eyes are always making tears? They are washing over the front of each eyeball all the time, keeping it clean and dust-free. When you cry your eyes make extra liquid, which spills out and runs down your cheeks.

Your eyelids and lashes keep pieces of dirt out of your eyes. Tears wash your eyes clean. A tear duct in the corner of each eye drains into your nose.

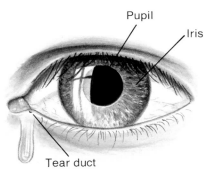

Pupil

Iris

Tear duct

 DO YOU KNOW

The iris is the colored part of the eye. The most common color is brown, then blue. The iris opens and closes to control the amount of light entering the eyeball. That's why pupils are big in dim light and small in bright light.

What is color blindness?

There are two main kinds of light-sensitive cells in the retina. Rods work in dim light and "see" in black and white. Cones pick up color, but only in bright light. People who are color blind cannot tell the difference between certain colors because some of their cone cells aren't working properly.

 DO YOU KNOW

Few women are color blind, but around 1 in 12 men can't see some colors properly.

The most common form of color blindness is not being able to tell red from green.

When do we grow fastest?

We grew fastest before we were born. In the nine months we spent in our mother's womb, we grew from a single cell no bigger than a period into a baby about 20 inches long and weighing 6 to 8 pounds. Babies go on growing quickly. By the time they are one year old, they are about four times as heavy as when they were born. By the time girls are $7\frac{1}{2}$ and boys are 9, they have reached three quarters of their adult height.

DO YOU KNOW

After about 20 weeks in the womb, the baby can hear sounds, tell light from dark, swallow, and suck its thumb. Some unborn babies even have the hiccups!

1 Twelve weeks after conception, the baby's brain, heart, and other main parts have already formed. The baby weighs only $\frac{1}{2}$ ounce and is about 2.5 inches long.

2 After 22 weeks the baby is tiny (11 inches long), but fully formed. For some time now it has been moving around a lot, and the mother sometimes feels it kicking.

3 After 34 weeks the baby weighs about 5.5 pounds and is roughly 18 inches long.

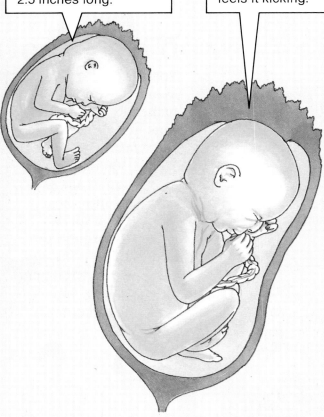

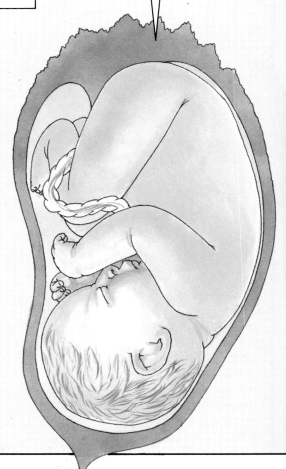

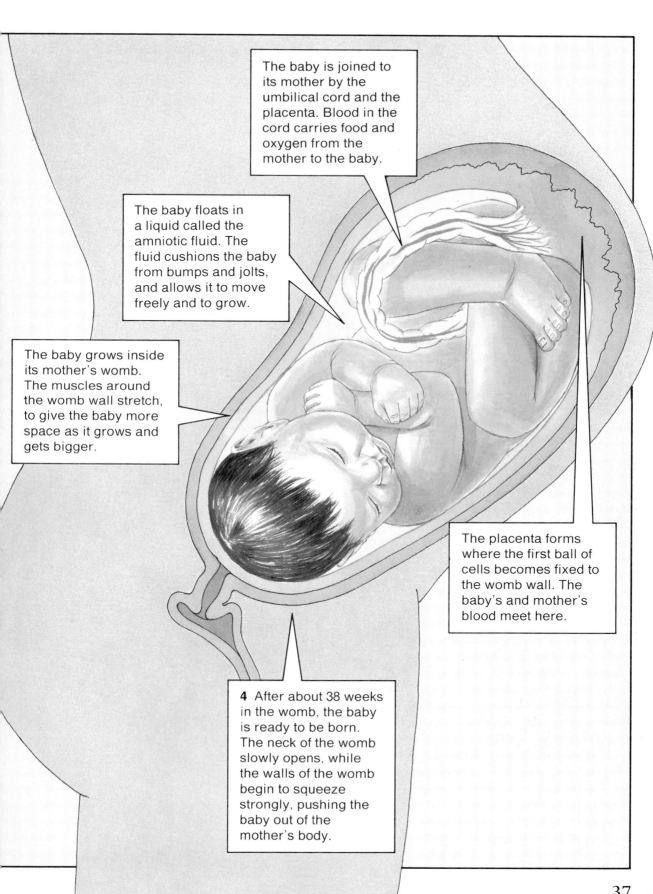

The baby is joined to its mother by the umbilical cord and the placenta. Blood in the cord carries food and oxygen from the mother to the baby.

The baby floats in a liquid called the amniotic fluid. The fluid cushions the baby from bumps and jolts, and allows it to move freely and to grow.

The baby grows inside its mother's womb. The muscles around the womb wall stretch, to give the baby more space as it grows and gets bigger.

The placenta forms where the first ball of cells becomes fixed to the womb wall. The baby's and mother's blood meet here.

4 After about 38 weeks in the womb, the baby is ready to be born. The neck of the womb slowly opens, while the walls of the womb begin to squeeze strongly, pushing the baby out of the mother's body.

What happens as we grow old?

As we grow old our bodies start to wear out and slow down. Our hair turns white, and our skin loses its stretchiness. Our muscles become weaker, and we can't move as fast. Our bones become harder and break more easily, and our joints become stiffer. Growing old is not all bad news, though. Most people go on leading active and happy lives – and the longer we live, the longer we have to learn about life and ourselves.

DO YOU KNOW

As we get older our cells renew themselves more slowly, so it takes longer to repair and replace parts of the body. This is the main reason why our bodies start to wear out as we get older.

AGE FACTS

● Many people live to be over 100 years old. The oldest known person lived for nearly 121 years.

● A dog is very old at 15 years, but a human being isn't very old until he or she is about 80.

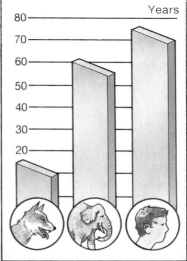

Useful words

Artery   Any blood vessel which carries blood away from the heart to the rest of the body.

Backbone   Also called the spine. The column of 26 bones (called vertebrae) which runs down the back. It encloses and protects the large bundle of nerve cells called the spinal cord.

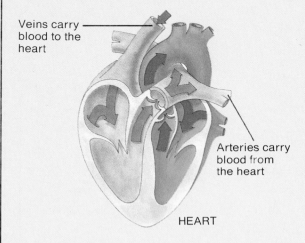

Veins carry blood to the heart

Arteries carry blood from the heart

HEART

Blood vessels   Tubes that carry the blood which the heart pumps around the body. Blood vessels that carry blood away from the heart are called arteries. Veins are the blood vessels that carry blood to the heart.

Cell   This is the body's smallest living unit, and the building block from which everything in the body is made. There are lots of different types of cells – blood cells, skin cells, nerve cells, muscle cells, for example. Each type does one particular job. An adult's body has about 50 billion cells in it.

Muscle   Muscles make the different parts of the body move. We can control some muscles by thinking about them – the ones in our arms and legs, for example. Others, such as the heart, work on their own.

Nerve   Nerves are special cells which carry messages to and from every part of the body to the brain. The messages travel along the nerves as tiny electrical currents.

Organ   A body part which does one particular job. The eye is an organ of sight, for example.

Oxygen   We take this gas into our bodies when we breathe air into our lungs – air is about 21% oxygen. Our bodies need oxygen to make energy and keep us alive. Without oxygen we would die.

Senses   We have five senses – hearing, sight, smell, taste, and touch.

Skeleton   The framework of bones which supports the body and carries its weight.

Vein   Any blood vessel which carries blood toward the heart.

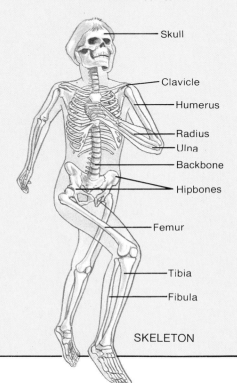

Skull
Clavicle
Humerus
Radius
Ulna
Backbone
Hipbones
Femur
Tibia
Fibula

SKELETON

Index